Meetings
secrets

The experts tell all!

About the author
Martin Manser has been a
professional reference book
editor since 1980. He has
compiled or edited more than
200 reference books, particularly
English-language dictionaries,
Bible-reference titles and
business skills books. Since 2001
he has also been a trainer and
consultant with national and
international companies and
organizations, leading courses on
Business Communication,
Effective Presentations, Time
Management, Running Effective
Meetings and Report Writing.
Among his books are *Presenting*
and *Time Management*, also in
the **business secrets** series.

Visit the author's website:
martinmanser.co.uk

Meetings
secrets

William Collins
An imprint of HarperCollins*Publishers*
1 London Bridge Street
London SE1 9GF

www.WilliamCollinsBooks.com

This Collins paperback edition published in Great Britain by William Collins in 2020

First published in Great Britain in 2020 by HarperCollins*Publishers*
Published in Canada by HarperCollins*Canada*. www.harpercollins.ca
Published in Australia by HarperCollins*Australia*. www.harpercollins.au
Published in India by *HarperCollinsPublishersIndia*. www.harpercollins.co.in

1

A catalogue record for this book
is available from the British Library

ISBN 978-0-00-838989-5

Typeset by Palimpsest Book Production Limited, Falkirk, Stirlingshire
Printed and bound by CPI Group (UK) Ltd, Croydon CR0 4YY

MIX
Paper from
responsible sources
FSC™ C007454
www.fsc.org

This book is produced from independently certified FSC™ paper
to ensure responsible forest management.

For more information visit: www.harpercollins.co.uk/green

Contents

Learn how to run an effective meeting

Meetings! Think how many business meetings you've been to. It's very easy to focus on the negative side of how time has been wasted and colleagues have been discouraged. The aim of this book, however, is to help you move ahead positively and to suggest ways in which you can make meetings even more useful.

I write as someone who has chaired meetings, taken minutes and sat as an active participant in countless meetings in the business world and also in schools and charities over the last four decades. But I also write as one who is not a natural leader, even though I have been called upon to chair meetings, take the minutes (sometimes at the same time as chairing!), so I have learnt certain skills. It is these that I want to pass on to you: if I have learnt to do it, I believe you can too.

This book contains 50 **secrets** of success, spread over seven chapters. These are:

1 **Why have meetings?** We begin by asking the basic question. What is the purpose of meetings? Meetings cost money: how much? It is important to know what are the different roles that colleagues have.

2 Prepare well for meetings. You need to make sure that all the practical arrangements have been made but you also need to spend time preparing yourself for the meeting. If an important part of the meeting is negotiating, then you need to give special attention to preparing for that, too.

3 Chairing a meeting. The chair's role is vital in ensuring that the meeting runs well and achieves its aim by guiding it skilfully, providing direction, making progress and reaching decisions firmly.

4 Taking minutes. To write the minutes of a meeting, you need to develop certain skills, such as listening well and noting the relevant points. You will then be able to write them up effectively after the meeting.

5 Giving a presentation. If the thought of giving a presentation at a meeting fills you with dread, then you need to follow the steps given here to relieve your fears and help you become more confident.

6 Taking part in a meeting. Everyone has a role to play in the meeting, even if you're not the chair or minute-taker. You can make a positive contribution by participating fully, listening well, discussing positively, speaking persuasively and negotiating successfully.

7 After the meeting. Even though the meeting has finished, that isn't the end. You need to build on all your preparation and hard work to ensure that the actions are followed through well and that the work makes good progress.

Whatever your role in a meeting, you can become more confident.

Why have meetings?

There are many different kinds of meeting: for example, an appraisal to consider individual performance and set goals and targets for the future, a team meeting to consider the work of the team, a conference at which experts give papers on a specialist subject, or a large Annual General Meeting to review a year's work in a company or organization.

But whatever their format or length, meetings all have certain features in common: you need to know their purpose, prepare for them carefully, conduct them well and follow them up effectively for them to be considered successful.

1.1

Know your purpose

It may seem unnecessary to discuss the purpose of meetings, but it is a question that has probably occurred to you when you are in the middle of a long, boring meeting: 'Why am I here? What are we actually achieving?' So before the meeting starts, you need to work out what you want to achieve during the meeting.

Asking 'What is the purpose of this meeting?' is probably the most important question that you can ask as you plan, prepare for or go into a meeting: what is its aim? What exactly are you trying to achieve? One thing is certain: if you don't know the purpose of your meeting before you begin it, it's unlikely that you'll achieve a purpose while the meeting is taking place and before it ends. Further, how will you know if the meeting had been successful if you don't know what you're aiming to achieve?

Here are some possible aims of meetings:

■ to give information, e.g. to inform colleagues of progress or introduce new products or services
■ to review progress on a project
■ to negotiate details of a contract

■ to negotiate arrangements, e.g. financial or in politics
■ to discuss a proposal for a future project
■ to assess and evaluate different strategies or ways of dealing with a problem or a dispute
■ to review and approve a certain course of action or a set of accounts
■ to come to a decision on a proposal and agree what to do next
■ to choose new members of a committee, board, leadership group, etc.
■ to listen to or give a talk or presentation on a subject
■ to develop a sense of team identity and encourage more effective teamwork

Keep the aims of your meeting simple and clear.

1.2

What can go wrong in meetings?

If we look at some of the things that can go wrong in a meeting, then we can learn from mistakes.

- inappropriate time of meeting, e.g. just before the end of the day
- the meeting is called at short notice
- poor or no agenda
- unclear purpose of meeting
- spending time during the meeting reading background reports
- not having enough copies of papers or reports for all participants
- participants arrive late
- wrong people present
- people who have authority to make decisions are not present
- unclear roles
- noisy venue; room too hot or too cold
- seating unhelpful for discussion
- some people talk too much; others talk too little

case study Larry was called in to solve the problems at the company. He was present at a meeting of the Senior Management Team (SMT). He asked them for the agenda of the meeting and was told there wasn't one. He asked them for the actions decided at the previous meeting and was told that no minutes had

- participants are not prepared
- no follow-up from previous meeting
- participants do not reach conclusions or decisions
- participants do not decide actions or who is responsible for them
- poor or no chair
- discussion is in too much detail
- meeting goes on too long: no breaks
- new people present but no one introduces them
- participants use jargon that is not known to all participants
- participants do not really listen to one another
- participants talk to each other during the meeting
- distractions during the meeting, e.g. mobile phones ringing
- participants not being open to change their minds
- participants misinterpret others' comments
- disagreement or conflict becomes personal
- too many people are talking at the same time
- technical issues
- decisions poorly communicated after the meeting

Most of these can be solved by:

- better chairing of the meeting
- better preparation before the meeting.

Most of the problems with meetings can be solved by better preparation.

been taken. It was hardly surprising that the company was in a complete mess. Fortunately, Larry knew members of the SMT well, so he could make changes easily and put structures in place, so within a few months the company was making good progress.

1.3

Calculate the cost of meetings

Let's stand back and look at how much meetings actually cost. Suppose there are eight managers in a meeting that lasts three hours. How much do you think the meeting will cost?

Suppose each manager's salary is £30,000.

£30,000 ÷ 48 (52 weeks in the year minus 4 for holidays) = £625 per week.

£625 ÷ 5 = £125 per day. So £125 is what each manager receives as gross pay per day, before tax or other deductions.

Now let's work out the hourly rate of pay received. Managers may be in the office for seven hours but how many of those are actually productive? Let's say five so we have £125 ÷ 5 = £25 per hour: this is the amount of gross pay that a manager is paid per hour.

But we need to multiply £25 by approximately 3 (some colleagues have suggested 2.7; others have suggested 5) to account for general business expenses. We need to think not only of the salaries of those concerned but also of the general costs to the company or organization of each individual's time. Someone has to pay for electricity, cleaning, buildings and employees' insurance, and government taxes. These could be allocated to each individual. Such general business expenses are referred to as overheads.

"Time is money"

Benjamin Franklin (1706–90), American statesman, scientist and author: *Advice to a Young Tradesman* (1748)

one minute wonder In a meeting, I sometimes think that I'm in a taxi and I'm watching the meter go up minute by minute for the fare I will be charged. I can see that time costs money. In the same way, meetings cost money.

£25 pounds x 3 = £75. So £75 is the cost per hour of one manager. Now suppose the meeting lasts three hours and eight managers attend it, then the cost of the meeting is £75 x 3 ×8 = £1800.

This figure is probably higher than you thought.

It also has certain effects: suppose seven managers are waiting for one manager who is 10 minutes late. The amount of money that is wasted while waiting for the late colleague is £88, i.e. £75 ÷ 6 (for 10 minutes) x 6 colleagues = £75.

Suppose also that during the meeting the chairman says that time did not allow them to circulate the paper in advance so every member of the meeting now has to spend 5 minutes reading through the paper, then that costs £75 ÷ 12 (for 5 minutes) x 8 = £50.

This means that you should keep your meetings as short as possible to avoid wasting resources.

Keep your meetings as short as possible to avoid wasting resources.

1.4

Who makes decisions in meetings?

Who is responsible for making a decision in your company or organization?

It can be helpful to consider who it is that makes decisions in a meeting: do all colleagues or only some colleagues make the decisions?

The acronym **RACI** can be used in this discussion.

■ **R** those who are **Responsible**: the colleagues who will be actually doing the task.

■ **A** those who are **Accountable**: those with ultimate authority for the decision, and who could be blamed if it goes wrong.

■ **C** those who are **Consulted**: those colleagues, e.g. consultants, who can give expert advice or others affected by the decision – for instance, those involved in a project or certain stakeholders, such as suppliers or trade unions. Such colleagues are consulted about decisions but do not actually make the decisions themselves.

■ **I** those who are **Informed**: colleagues who only need to be informed about the decisions that have already been made, but need not be consulted and are not responsible for making the actual decision.

Some authorities also add **O** for **Omit** for those colleagues who do not need to be informed or consulted about the decision and are not responsible for it, to make the acronym **CAIRO** (**C**onsulted, **A**ccountable, **I**nformed, **R**esponsible, **O**mit).

The significance of this is that time can be wasted and roles confused unless it is clear who it is that actually makes the decision.

You should also consider how decisions are made in your company or organization:

■ Are decisions made by the leader? This can often be quick and efficient but could be considered harsh as colleagues may not have been involved and may not feel valued as their views are not sought.
■ Are decisions made by a majority? This can be considered fair but the minority may be reluctant to put the decision into action.
■ Are decisions made by general agreement (consensus)? This has the disadvantage that it may take a long time to win over each colleague but it has the advantage that colleagues will feel committed to putting them into action as they have been part of the decision-making process.

It is important to be clear about who makes the decision. If you are not clear on this, roles may become confused and time will be wasted.

1.5

Know the different roles

It is important to know the different roles that need to be fulfilled to make sure that a meeting runs smoothly.

The key roles in a meeting are:

■ **The chair**, who works with other colleagues to help prepare the agenda, welcomes newcomers, builds good relationships with participants, keeps the meeting on track and reviews progress, stimulates discussion, summarizes and then makes decisions. This role is important and we devote a whole section to this: see pages 36–51.

■ **The coordinator/secretary**, who plans the venue and time, invites the relevant participants, agrees the agenda with the chair, sends out the agenda and any papers and reports before the meeting, prepares the room for the meeting and makes arrangements for refreshments, etc.

■ **The minute-taker**, who will work with the chair to ensure that a full statement of what is agreed at the meeting is recorded. The minute-taker will not write down every word, just significant matters, and will write up the minutes as soon as possible after the meeting, check with the chair that they accurately reflect the content of the meeting and send out the minutes as soon as possible after the meeting. Again this role is crucial and we devote a whole section to this: see pages 52–63.

■ Every participant has a role to play in the meeting by preparing themselves and reading the material in advance of the meeting and listening well and responding positively. If you leave a meeting thinking that it was a waste of time, then you are partly responsible: each person has a role to play.

When you are next in a meeting in which you do not feel involved, think of what you can do positively to move the meeting on … and do it.

Whatever your role – chair, coordinator/secretary, minute-taker or participant – each person has an important role to play to make sure that the meeting is successful.

Prepare well for meetings

How many meetings have you been to where things have gone wrong? Has a room where you'd planned to hold the meeting been double-booked? Have you ever arrived at a venue and no one is expecting you? Have you ever arrived at the wrong time? Or if you are in the meeting, and the seating is poorly laid out, the relevant people are not present; there is no agenda, and papers and reports have not been circulated before the meeting ... Unfortunately, the list could go on and on. In this chapter we consider how to prepare well for meetings to make sure that they are successful and effective.

2.1

Make the practical arrangements

Preparation for a meeting is vital. What is the best time of day to hold it? For example, if you hold the meeting just before lunch then colleagues will want to finish punctually. If you hold it just after lunch they may be sleepy. Think what is the best time.

You also need to consider the venue:

■ If you are holding a conference, will you need several rooms, e.g. one formal room to conduct the official business and a separate room for refreshments? Will you need rooms for breakouts, small discussion groups? Book the rooms you need as soon as possible.

■ If you're considering an external venue, e.g. a hotel, then choose one that is easily accessible to most of your participants. Arrange an appointment with the on-site conference manager to discuss your requirements and their facilities and prices. If the venue is away from your offices, then check car parking and access to public transport.

---

case study Jane and Kate needed some quiet time to think through their strategy for a forthcoming project so they booked room A3 in their offices from 9.30 a.m. Unfortunately, they had only booked that room

■ If you are having an appraisal or are discussing a sensitive matter, then consider meeting at a neutral venue. Try to arrange the seating so that you sit at right angles to the person you are speaking to. Further, the chair you are sitting on should be at the same level as the person you are speaking to.

Also list the basics:

■ How many participants are attending.
■ How you want the seating to be laid out in the room. Examples: horseshoe (U-shaped) seating, if you want all participants to have good eye contact with one another; boardroom-style seating where participants sit around a long table; conference- or theatre-style seating in which speakers sit in a row in front of the audience; cabaret/restaurant-style seating for more informal occasions.
■ Whether refreshments are needed and if so when and what; don't forget special dietary requirements.
■ The lighting and air-conditioning/heating of the room.
■ Wi-Fi availability (e.g. password for access to the Internet).
■ Other equipment that you will require.
■ Facilities for those hard of hearing and/or with special access requirements.
■ Accessibility to toilets.

These lists may seem unimportant but you only have to forget one detail to realize that working through a check list is essential.

for an hour, so at 10.30 a.m., just as they were making good progress, some other colleagues interrupted them saying they had booked the room from 10.30 a.m. The lesson: check your arrangements.

2.2

Invite the relevant people

Have you ever been at a meeting where you all look at each other and realize that the person who is most needed at the meeting isn't present? You need to take care over inviting the relevant participants to attend the meeting.

To invite participants:

■ Check their availability on your computer system or contact them by phone or email to see if they're available. If the meeting is a regular one, for example of a subcommittee, then there will be little choice over who to invite. However, if the meeting is taking place only on that occasion, then you need to take certain steps. Begin by checking that the most important person/people can attend. Confirm their availability in an email so there is no doubt later. If you want people to attend only the part of a meeting that is relevant to them, then make that clear.

■ Invite those participants who need to attend. Some people suggest that you should invite many people on the basis of not wanting to offend those who are not invited. However, if you have too many participants, then the discussion is likely to last a long time and it will be difficult to reach decisions. (On the other hand, if you invite too few people, then those who are present may complain that other people's interests are not being heard and so consider that the meeting lacks authority.)

■ If you are in doubt about who to invite, then check who was present at similar meetings in the past and/or discuss the choice with the chairs of other meetings to make sure you do not exclude anyone essential.

■ It is good to have a mix of people, i.e. you do not want all the participants to agree with one another. Disagreements can sometimes be a healthy way to help refine the road ahead.

■ Send an email confirming the following:

- The date and time of the meeting (start time and likely finish time) and the venue. You may want to invite them to come a few minutes before the meeting if refreshments are available.
- The subject of the meeting and any agenda and papers to be read (these could be sent at a later date but should still be sent well before the meeting). If the person is expected to lead discussion on a particular point, then confirm that, too. If they want to use a PowerPoint presentation, then ask them to bring it on their own laptop and also on a memory stick (saved in an earlier version of PowerPoint in case their laptop fails and you need to use another one).
- Directions to the venue, with links to maps or notes on car parking or access by public transport.
- A request to let you know of any special requirements.
- Your contact details, including on the day, e.g. if their train is late they can still contact you on your mobile and not be put through to an office voicemail.
- If relevant, guidelines on dress code.

Ask the people you invite to confirm they can attend by a certain date, e.g. so that you can finalize numbers for catering purposes.

2.3

Plan an agenda

The agenda is the list of items to be discussed at the meeting. It should be circulated to those attending the meeting well in advance, together with any relevant papers or reports to be discussed during the meeting.

You should include the following in the agenda:

■ The name of the committee, etc., of the company or organization.
■ The date and time of the meeting and the venue.
■ A list of the members who will attend the meeting. My preference is to list these in the following order to show the roles of the individuals: Ray Smith (chair), then every other individual with their job title listed either in terms of seniority (the highest/most important coming first) or in alphabetical order of their family name. The name of the person taking the minutes should also be given.
■ Apologies (this means any individuals who should be present at the meeting but who cannot attend will have their apologies noted).
■ Regular items such as:

- **Minutes of the previous meeting held on [insert date].** This is the opportunity for the minutes of the previous meeting to be approved and signed as a correct record.
- **Matters arising.** These are matters that have arisen from the previous minutes but are not listed on the present agenda.
- **Financial reports and other progress reports.**

■ New items to be discussed at the meeting. Here, it is useful for the most important items to be discussed as soon as possible, rather than being left to the end.

- Don't try to fit too many items of significant new business into the meeting.
- The final item on the agenda should ideally be positive, to avoid participants leaving the meeting in a negative mood.

Two items often come at the end of the agenda:

■ **AOB (any other business).** This is the opportunity for individuals at the meeting to raise other items to discuss. However, participants should ideally not raise significant items without informing the chair before the meeting.

■ **DONM (date of next meeting).** To arrange the date of the next meeting of the committee, group, etc.

Agendas also sometimes include the following:

■ the name of the individual (or their initials) who will lead the discussion of a particular point;

■ the length of time that a particular point is planned to take.

Send out the agenda with a covering note well in advance of the meeting, to give participants enough time to prepare for it.

2.4

Prepare for a meeting

Before you go to your meeting, it is essential that you prepare for it.

I begin my preparation for an important meeting two days before the meeting itself. I do this for two reasons:

■ The start of my preparation might be delayed. If I begin my preparation only the day before the meeting and am delayed, then I will have no time to prepare for the meeting.

■ After I've completed my main preparation I often find that new thoughts occur to me. By allowing extra time before the meeting, I give my subconscious mind the opportunity to raise thoughts.

Here are four steps in your preparation for a meeting:

1 **Read through the papers circulated in advance** and consider what your thoughts are on the issues to be discussed. Write down your thoughts on the agenda or on a separate sheet of paper. Don't think that you will remember the points in your mind; you may remember them only for a few seconds or minutes but not for a day or two.

2 **Take time to arrange your papers** in order of the items to be discussed at the meeting. If there are several sheets of paper on many different issues, you could collect the papers together

"To fail to prepare is to prepare to fail"
Benjamin Franklin

for each different point and clearly put the number of the point on the agenda on the first sheet. I sometimes also use coloured sheets of paper to separate the various points. All these methods are ways of saving time during the meeting itself. If some matters are repeated under different points, then you could even make additional photocopies for yourself so that all the information is readily accessible during the meeting.

3 **If you are working electronically,** then make sure that all the documents are readily available to you. During the meeting other participants will not have time to wait for you to open several documents on your laptop.

4 **Check the time and venue** and make sure you allow sufficient time to reach the venue.

In your preparation, read through the papers circulated in advance, think about the issues and write down your thoughts.

2.5

Prepare for negotiations

Negotiation is one aspect of a meeting that you need to pay special attention to in preparation.

Here are some steps you need to undertake in your preparation:

■ **Know the position of the other side.** You may not know this in detail but you should discover as much as you can about them. What is the company's background? Are they strong or weak? What are their aims? Where are they positioned in the industry? What is important to them? What dealings have you had with them in the past? Do they really need your product/service?

- Note also that the person you are dealing with in the negotiations may not be the person in the company or organization who has the authority to make the final decision.

■ **Know your own position.**

- Do you really believe in the product/service you are offering? Is it unique or 'me too'?
- Which factors are negotiable and which non-negotiable?
- What precisely are you offering?
- What are the highest and lowest points you are willing to accept?

For example, if you are delivering books you might be willing to negotiate on the schedule but not on the price you want to sell the books for.

- Work out in advance the range that you are willing to discuss; for example, if you're negotiating price then the best price might be x and the worst y.

■ **Know what you want to achieve.** On which points is there likely to be agreement? And on which is there likely to be disagreement?

- Think about possible objections the other side might raise to your proposal and how you will respond to each of them.
- Work out in advance the benefits and advantages your product/service will bring them.
- What are the range of options that you are willing to accept, e.g. highest/lowest price, earliest/latest delivery times?
- Work out the financial terms you would ideally like to agree.
- Consider what alternatives you can offer if the other side refuses to accept what you offer.

■ **Work out the process** you are going to adopt:

- What will be your opening offer?
- At what point will you be willing to make a concession?
- How many points are you willing to concede?

■ **Negotiating as a team.** If you're working as a team, agree among yourselves what you will offer and the points you will and will not compromise on.

If the other side is well prepared and you're not, then they are sure to win.

2.6

On the day of the meeting

A meeting can be ruined by neglecting small details, so it is important to build on all your careful preparation by checking a whole range of points on the day of the meeting before it actually starts.

It is important for you to arrive well before the meeting starts. It is also possible that someone who has travelled a long distance will arrive a long time before the meeting starts (and those who have far less distance to travel will sometimes be late!).

■ Check the room: is the seating as you asked for? If you want to walk around the room is there enough space behind the chairs for you to do so?
■ Is the room itself clean; are all the tables clear of unnecessary papers? Is the lighting working all right? Is the heating/air conditioning adequate? Are there waste-paper bins? They should be empty.

---

case study John arrived late at the venue. He had forgotten to order a taxi in advance and had to wait around in the hotel lobby for a while. When he eventually arrived, the participants on the course were wondering if he would ever come at all. And as he began to set up his things in the room, he discovered that the projector he had asked for wasn't there. So

---

■ If refreshments are being served to participants, offer a choice of varieties of tea and coffee and any light refreshments such as biscuits or pastries and fruit.

■ Check the exact times for the serving of refreshments and any meals. Double-check that any special dietary requirements are being dealt with satisfactorily.

■ If participants are coming to a conference, are the binders of notes put out for each delegate? With notepad and pen? Post-it notes? Highlighter pens can also be useful.

■ Put out water and glasses for participants.

■ Check the projector, screen and flip chart and whiteboard. Link up your laptop to the projector to make sure it works and put on the opening slide of your presentation. Check the power cables are safe.

■ Check that a spare set of flip-chart paper is available. Test the flip-chart and whiteboard pens to see they still work (and keep them separate: permanent ink cannot be erased easily). I usually carry a spare set of flip-chart pens with me when leading a course.

■ Check your list of participants so that you can sign them in when they arrive. You may also want to supply name badges.

■ Note the location of the fire exits and the route to the assembly point. Find out if fire alarms are to be tested that day and if so, at what time.

■ Note the location of toilets and other facilities, e.g. prayer rooms for men and women.

A meeting that has been well prepared for is more likely to be successful.

everyone had to wait around for another half an hour while the technician came and fixed up the laptop, projector and screen. A while later, the fire alarm went off; fortunately it was a false alarm but he lost another valuable fifteen minutes. The subject of the course: time management!

Chairing a meeting

We turn now to the role of the chair.[1] The chair's role is crucial: he or she is the leader of the meeting, and should guide it carefully, setting its tone well. A good chair will not be distracted or diverted but will provide direction and reach decisions firmly.

In this chapter we also consider what to do when the meeting has become set in its ways and how you can introduce change. Finally, we look at what qualities and skills you need to become an effective chair.

1 The word 'chair' indicates a chairman or chairwoman, i.e. male or female.

3.1

Before the meeting

The chair's work doesn't begin when the meeting starts. As chair, you need to work hard before the meeting to make sure everything is in place so that it will run smoothly and be successful.

If you're chairing the meeting, then before it starts you should:

■ Work out with the secretary/coordinator:

- who should attend the meeting
- when the meeting should be held
- where the meeting should be held
- what needs to be discussed and put on the agenda so that it can be circulated before the meeting
- ensure that the relevant additional papers and reports are circulated before the meeting
- advise on other arrangements, e.g. seating, provision and timing of refreshments (but delegate implementing these details)
- ensure that you're sitting in a position where you can see all the participants and they can see you

case study A particular point had proved controversial in the large weekly meeting. Gillian therefore decided to have a quiet word with the two key individuals who had disagreed in the meeting. It turned out

■ Liaise with the minute-taker to make sure that the main aims of the meeting are clear and if there are likely to be any difficulties.
■ Arrive early to make sure all the arrangements are in place.

The above are the details, and in my experience it's easy to become so preoccupied with them that you don't pay enough attention to the main thing:

■ Know before the meeting what purpose you want to achieve during the meeting. This is the main point: where do you want to end up? For example, do you want all your colleagues to have agreed to take a decision in principle and spend a certain amount of money?

Before the meeting, you may also want to discuss with key individuals topics that are on the agenda and are likely to be controversial. In such conversations, you can prepare colleagues – and yourself – for how the discussion may proceed during the meeting. Time spent doing this isn't wasted.

Don't become so taken up with the details that you forget the main purpose that you want to achieve in the meeting.

that the issue was relatively minor. But because Gillian had settled the issue between meetings, the next meeting could pursue the real agenda and make good progress.

3.2

Guide the meeting skilfully

The chair's role is to keep the meeting on track and ensure it is not diverted or distracted.

During the meeting, as chair you should:

■ Sit somewhere where you can see all the participants in the meeting and they can see you.

■ Be ordered and disciplined, e.g. start and end the meeting on time and take a firm line on distractions, e.g. the use of mobile phones during the meeting.

■ Greet participants, welcome newcomers and as necessary get participants to introduce themselves.

■ State the overall purpose of the meeting: this vital step is often missed out but it is essential to set the tone of the meeting and to establish clearly the main aim in everyone's mind.

■ Ensure that the follow-up points from the previous meeting have been actioned satisfactorily.

■ Maintain order and control of the meeting, keep the meeting on track, e.g. making sure that only one person speaks at a time and that participants stick to the point.

■ Be as objective and impartial as possible.

■ Keep good relationships among the participants, e.g. by valuing each contribution.

■ Listen well to who is speaking and who isn't. A good chair will bring out quieter participants and as necessary gently but firmly quieten down those who are constantly vocal.

■ Notice participants' body language; for example, if they are bored.

As chair, introduce new points or ask a colleague to speak. Your role as chair is to make sure that the points to be discussed – and also the order in which they are to be discussed – are clear, e.g. explaining what an issue is before discussing solutions.

The chair should:

■ Stimulate discussion by asking questions. This can be more helpful than simply stating, 'Let's hear your responses to this idea.' Avoid questions that produce a direct 'yes' or 'no' answer. Choose open-ended questions, e.g. 'Why do we think that idea is worth pursuing?' Work hard at making your questions brief and simple.

■ Offer additional views and note possible effects ('If we follow that line, then we would be setting a precedent ... is that what we want to do?').

■ Review, summarize and make decisions (see Secret 3.4) at the end of points.

■ Allow all the participants to speak on a particular point even if you don't agree with them.

Make sure that you know the basic level of participants' understanding of the subjects being discussed. I once spoke at length only to find out I was speaking far above the participants' understanding.

3.3

Get out of a rut

Sometimes the discussion in a meeting 'goes round and round in circles', that is, nothing significant is achieved because participants keep coming back to the same points or problems over and over again. How can this be resolved? As chair, you need to give direction and take a strong lead.

Here are some practical ways of solving this problem.

■ The chair needs to:

- identify the key issues involved
- allow discussion of the various points concerned with the issues
- make proposals that respond to the key issues
- gain agreement using the method of decision-making appropriate to that group

■ Have a short agenda with only the significant issues on it.
■ Set a time limit for discussing the particular points.
■ Set up a subgroup to consider the particular issue in greater depth, make conclusions and recommendations, and report back to the next meeting.

"Any committee is only as good as the most knowledgeable, determined and vigorous person on it. There must be somebody who provides the flame"

Claudia (Lady Bird) Johnson (1912–2007),
widow of former US President, Lyndon B Johnson

■ Before the meeting takes place, prepare suggestions as to resolving the issue. Put these on the agenda: this means that time does not need to be spent suggesting the proposals in the meeting itself. Instead, time can be spent discussing the proposals that have already been set out. Further, the chair can contact the key participants of the meeting before it, find out their views and prepare them for the proposals at it.

The chair needs to give direction and take a strong lead to move discussion on.

3.4

Come to a decision firmly

As chair, you need to lead the meeting to reach decisions. What steps will you take in the decision-making process?

■ **Define the central issue.** Sometimes this is difficult. For example, your computer systems might be old but the real issue might be a lack of communication between certain colleagues in the IT department and other departments. You need to clarify what the real issue is. Also:

- consider when the decision needs to be made by. Try not to let an imminent deadline affect the quality of the decision-making process
- obtain relevant information to help you consider the issues: what is the context/background of the core issue? Why has it arisen?
- consult experts and defer a decision to a later meeting

■ **Identify** a range of alternative ideas and ways that deal with the central issue that you have defined.

- think creatively; challenge assumptions
- consider the cost of different options

"Be willing to make decisions. That's the most important quality in a good leader"

George S. Patton (1885–1945), American General

■ **Evaluate the range of alternatives.** If you're considering, for example, six different computer systems, reduce the number to a short-list of three.

- set up certain objective criteria by which you will assess the different options
- consider the effects of choosing each option: the advantages and disadvantages of each; the costs, benefits and risks
- consider where your resources can be used most effectively
- consider the timing and the order of different events in a process
- don't ignore your intuitions

■ **Note** that indecision – not making a decision – is also a decision in itself. This recalls the French philosopher Jean Buridan who considered the idea of a donkey that finds itself unable to choose between two equally attractive bales of hay and so starves to death.

■ **Make the decision.**

- work out the effects of the decision: who will do what and by what date
- decisions should be SMART (see Secret 3.5)
- communicate the decision to other relevant colleagues and implement it

Have the courage to make the right decision.

3.5

Have SMART action points

It's no use having action points that are vague and unrealistic. Define your action points clearly to make sure they are realistic.

Action points should be **SMART**:

■ **Specific** – not vague, but clear and precise. State in plain terms what you want to achieve. Focus exactly on what you want to do. The temptation in a meeting is to be vague, not precise. For example, 'We hope to increase our profits within the next two years' isn't specific, but vague. Far better is: 'We will increase our profits by £1 million by the end of next year.'

■ **Measurable** – so that you can assess the progress you are making ... or not making. You could set certain key performance indicators (KPIs); for example, setting a certain percentage of income as coming from existing customers.

■ **Agreed** – by all the people present. This is important, because you don't want to have the situation later when one colleague states, 'I never supported that project anyway.' If everyone in a meeting agrees on a course of action, then everyone should support that decision after the meeting.

"If you don't know where you are going, you will probably end up somewhere else"

Laurence J. Peter (1919–90), Canadian educator, and Raymond Hull (1919–85), playwright: *The Peter Principle* (1969)

■ **Realistic** – that may stretch you but not be so completely beyond your reach that they are unrealistic and unattainable.

■ **Timed** – with a definite time for completion, to help you fulfil your commitment by beginning to take action now.

Some authorities also add **ER**:

■ **Evaluated** – that you check on the progress as you move to complete your goals.

■ **Reported** – that are recorded, e.g. at a subsequent meeting.

Having precise action points focuses your attention and gives you clear aims to keep in sight.

3.6

Manage change well

The chair is called on to provide leadership: vision and direction. He or she will certainly influence and shape the thinking and actions of others. I sometimes think of a leader as the captain of a ship, who sets a course for others to follow. Leaders lead people.

One important aspect of leadership is change. So one significant part of the role of the chair is to introduce change.

How does a leader introduce change?

■ Recognize that some colleagues will resist change. Most of us do not like change. We like to keep things the way they are. We may be satisfied with our present position and are unsure about the future. We know where we are with our present circumstances and structures. Change brings uncertainty.

■ Explain why change is necessary. It may be that your competitors have moved forward from you and have taken your market. Or perhaps new technology has come in, making your existing products or services less attractive. Explain that the changes are necessary to keep up with the times and to remain ahead of the competition.

■ Develop a sense of vision and a clear strategy. Don't be diverted or distracted from the new course that has been set. Communicate the fresh vision and strategy effectively to colleagues. Understand, and respond effectively to, the challenges involved in change.

"Leadership is about vision, about people buying in, about empowering people and, most of all, about producing useful change"

Dr John P. Kotter, American authority on leadership

■ Build strong relationships among and between colleagues that will build on the purpose and the strategy that have been developed, so that individuals will respond well to the changes being proposed.

■ Motivate colleagues, e.g. by giving them authority and the resources to implement the new strategy.

■ Realize it will take time to make significant changes in a company or organization. Try therefore to secure some 'quick wins'; that is, actions with immediate visible benefits and that can be implemented relatively easily and quickly.

In introducing change, you need to keep explaining why change is necessary.

3.7

Develop your skills as chair

What knowledge, skills and personal qualities do you need to become a good chair?

Knowledge, skills and personal qualities needed:

■ be able to plan ahead, rather than reacting to changes
■ remain focused on the important aim of achieving goals
■ be able to inspire others by your words and also your example
■ be an effective communicator; respect others; be objective; be able to motivate others, supporting and facilitating colleagues
■ be able to set clear strategic goals
■ be able to discern the real issues
■ be able to handle complex issues or diverse opinions
■ be good with finances, setting budgets and establishing systems that monitor and control expenditure

case study Over the years I've had to learn to become a chair. Being quiet in my natural personality, I found taking up the leadership role of a chair difficult. To begin with, I wasn't assertive enough in chairing meetings. Gradually I've learnt certain skills, such as standing up in front of others and speaking firmly, dealing with difficult people,

- be good at analysing information, both in words and numbers
- be decisive: having the ability to make decisions
- be diplomatic, able to rise above any 'hidden agenda'
- be confident
- be good at networking with others to develop trusted relationships
- be able to delegate clearly to trusted members of your team, empowering them, to avoid becoming stressed by taking too much on yourself
- be able to work well under pressure
- be a good team player, establishing clear roles
- be able to handle conflict well; be able to distinguish between what is negotiable and what is non-negotiable; be creative and flexible in finding solutions to difficulties; have good negotiation skills
- be a good listener, maintaining appropriate eye contact
- be able to see the big picture
- be able to keep track of different processes ('keep several balls in the air') at the same time; be able to document progress clearly
- have integrity; be trustworthy; keep confidentialities
- remember people's names
- be persistent in completing tasks reliably; be committed

If you are a chair, which of these qualities are you good at? Now choose one that you need to develop more. Discuss with a colleague what the next step is for you to do that.

not allowing distractions from the path I've believed to be right and at times taking unpopular decisions. It has taken courage but I have become more confident. I have developed my own style of chairing. I've learnt to think ahead and to know what is needed to guide people to reach a goal together.

Taking minutes

The minutes are the official record of who was present at a meeting, the decisions that were made and the action points to be followed up.

The role of minute-taker is therefore crucial.

If you've never taken minutes before, it can seem a daunting task. But relax – in the following pages I've broken down the task into easy-to-follow steps of what you need to do at every stage: from before the meeting starts to during the actual meeting and then after the meeting has finished. Finally, we consider what qualities and skills you need to become an effective minute-taker.

4.1

Before the meeting

The minute-taker's responsibility does not begin at the start of the meeting. As with many other aspects of running an effective meeting, you need to prepare yourself before the meeting to ensure that is successful.

The relationship between the chair and the minute-taker is important. One aspect of this is that the two of you should get together before the meeting to discuss:

■ the names of the participants who will attend the meeting
■ any technical aspects. The chair should explain any technical matters that you as minute-taker may be unfamiliar with
■ any abbreviations or acronyms (every company and organization has these!) that you may be unfamiliar with
■ the agenda and accompanying reports, especially any issues on which there is likely to be disagreement, so that you are particularly alert to these
■ the level of detail that the chair wants you as minute-taker to record, e.g. does the chair want all discussion points recorded, or simply the decisions reached? If discussion points are to be noted, then does the chair want the names of the individuals making those points to be part of the minutes or not?
■ the style of minutes that the chair wants you to use. This may mean simply using the previous minutes as a guide. It is especially important

to note how the chair wants the action points that are decided at the meeting to be noted
■ where both you and the chair will sit during the meeting. You must be able to make good eye contact with the chair. An ideal place is next to or very near each other

As minute-taker you also need to make sure you have an adequate supply of pens (ideally in different colours to highlight different aspects), pencils, and paper etc., if the draft of the minutes is to be on hard copy, or that your computer (laptop, iPad, etc.) is fully operational and ready for use if the minutes are being typed straight on to a computer.

You should arrive early for the meeting: see also Secret 2.6.

The relationship between the chair and the minute-taker is crucial.

4.2

During the meeting

This is the main part of your work as minute-taker.

During the meeting, as minute-taker you should:

■ note the date, time and venue of the meeting
■ record any apologies for absence that have been received
■ if the meeting is formal, draw up a seating plan showing which participant is seated where
■ use the agenda as the structure of your minutes
■ concentrate on what is going on, listening closely to the discussion You will find that different colleagues have different styles in expressing themselves
■ take clear and accurate notes of the points made and the decisions reached. Focus on the important ones as well as the details. Early on in your experience as a minute-taker you are likely to try to note everything as you are not sure what is significant and what is not, but gradually you will discern what is most important. (If you can, also discuss this with the chair before the meeting)
■ record the meeting at a level of detail previously agreed with the chair, e.g. a concise summary of the discussion points as well as decisions and, if the chair wants, the names of the colleagues to action the discussion points
■ note the decisions clearly (see Secret 3.5 on setting SMART action points), particularly such significant items as:

"Committee: a group of people who keep minutes and waste hours"

Anon

- the amount of money that has been agreed will be spent, together with any particular part of a budget that this is to come from
- the precise action to be undertaken
- the time (date) by which an action point is to be completed
- the colleague responsible for following up the action point, i.e. who will implement it
- any next step in a process

As we saw in Secret 4.1, it is important that the chair and the minute-taker should have a good working relationship with each other so that the chair can say to you at a particular point, 'Please could you minute the following ...' Moreover, if the chair has not clearly stated what has been decided, as minute-taker you should ask the chair, 'What would you like me to minute here?'

As minute-taker, you must carefully note the decisions that have been agreed.

4.3

After the meeting

As minute-taker, your work hasn't finished at the end of the meeting. Whether you draft the minutes on hard copy or computer, your role is to check what has been noted to make sure that the minutes accurately and correctly reflect what took place.

As minute-taker, you should:

■ Write up a final version of the minutes from your notes as soon as possible after the meeting. Ideally write them up within a day of the meeting, while the points are still fresh in your mind.
■ Summarize the points made at the meeting. If the discussion continued for a long time but it basically centred on two key issues (e.g. cost and timing), then explain those concisely rather than noting colleagues' general vague wordiness.
■ Pass to the chair your draft of the minutes so that they can check the

case study Peter admitted to himself that he found writing up the minutes of the meeting rather boring and unexciting. He had to make sense of pages of notes he had written during the meeting. But whenever he wrote up the minutes, he always remembered some detail he had not written down during the meeting. It

content. Note that the chair is unlikely to check basic things such as the date and venue of the meeting and its participants, so if you've used the minutes of a previous meeting as a basis, make sure you change the date!
■ When the chair has agreed the content of the minutes, then the minutes should be circulated to the relevant individuals. Such circulation should take place as soon as possible after the meeting, not immediately before the next meeting of that group. Colleagues may not implement their action points until they receive the minutes, so that is a further reason why the minutes should be circulated promptly.
■ On the details of what to write and how to express it, see Secret 4.4.
■ File the minutes in a physical place, e.g. in a ring binder and/or electronically in an accessible location in your company's or organization's computer files.
■ Shred any confidential papers that you no longer need.

Check the minutes carefully before sending them to the chair. If you don't find any errors, you've not checked them thoroughly enough!

was all hard work, and yet as he undertook this task he also found it satisfying. He enjoyed not only expressing the content of the meeting but also capturing something of its tone. He learnt to find the right words to reflect the discussion that had taken place.

Write up the minutes

You need to write up the minutes well because they form the official record of what took place and was decided.

The minutes of the meeting should consist of the following items:

■ The name of the group or committee (e.g. 'Working group for spring conference'), with venue and time.

■ A list of those people present at the meeting, with the chair listed first and then others in order of their family name together with any titles or who they represent.

■ Other items should then broadly follow the order in which they appeared on the agenda, e.g. Apologies for absence, Approval of minutes of previous meeting and then the main subjects of that meeting.

■ As discussed in Secret 4.2, note carefully the decisions that were agreed at the meeting. You may also (if the chair has indicated they want this) want to note a concise summary of the points discussed leading up to that decision. You will develop your own style: there is no one right way to write minutes. Keep your language objective and professional. Keep sentences short: about 15 words. Keep paragraphs short: four or five sentences.

Other words you could use instead of 'say': *agree, clarify, conclude, confirm, emphasize, explain, inform, mention, propose, recommend, report, respond, suggest, verify.*

When minuting a disagreement, write, for example: 'After some discussion...' or 'Some colleagues expressed their disagreement with this view.'

■ If items are discussed out of order, for example discussion is held on subject A and then subject B and then back to subject A, then the minutes of the meeting should link all the items A together, i.e. not be interrupted by the minutes of subject B.

■ The action points agreed. It is particularly important that these are clearly identified, especially the person who is to undertake the action, what precisely they are to do and the date by which they should complete the work, e.g. **Action: Charles Henson to fill in forms by 30 May.**

■ The date, time and place of the next meeting.

Write up the minutes as soon as possible after the meeting while the points are still fresh in your mind.

4.5

Develop your skills as minute-taker

You will grow in time in your experience as a minute-taker. As you take the minutes of meetings, your fears and worries will decrease and you will find that you grow in confidence.

To be a good minute-taker, you should:

■ be able to concentrate for a long time: you will discover that listening is hard work!
■ be a good listener
■ be able to write objectively, i.e. making sure that your personal opinion is not expressed in the minutes
■ be able to write clearly
■ have and maintain a good working relationship with the chair of the meeting
■ remember people's names
■ be good at summarizing, i.e. not noting in your final minutes everything that everyone has said, but a shorter version, summing up the main points
■ be accurate about details, e.g. note exactly what the chair says has been decided

- be willing to ask questions at the appropriate time if you don't know something: don't be afraid to do this
- be trustworthy: you will deal with confidential information, especially about finances and perhaps about your colleagues
- get on with people
- be good at assessing the tone of the meeting
- be willing not to receive much attention. People don't usually notice the colleague who is taking the minutes

Look at the above list. Choose three qualities that you posses and one that you need to work harder to achieve. Discuss with a colleague what the next step is for you to improve that one quality. Be SMART (see Secret 3.5).

Giving a presentation

You've been asked to give a presentation at next week's meeting. What is your reaction? Panic? Cancelling all your plans to give you some space to prepare?

Here are some guidelines to help you take control of yourself. As you work through the steps you will become more confident, develop your own natural style and you may even find yourself enjoying the experience of presenting.

5.1

Know the aims of your presentation

It's vital to know why you are giving your presentation. It's important that you can define the purpose of what you're presenting in one sentence. This will clarify what you should include – and what you should leave out.

When I started leading courses in communication I devised the acronym **AIR: Audience, Intention, Response.** So:

■ **Audience:** Who is the audience? What are they like? What do they already know about the subject? You can then make sure that what you are saying is suitable for their level.

- What are the attitudes or feelings of the audience likely to be towards the subject you are presenting?
- What expectations does the audience have of you as the presenter?
- Do members of the audience know one another? Do they have good relationships with one another?
- Will members of the audience be present at the meeting because they have to be there or because they want to be there?
- Are there any hidden agendas or underlying tensions that you should be aware of?

- Who are the decision makers in the audience? What are their opinions?

■ Intention: What is the message you want to communicate? What are your key points? If you aren't clear on these, you cannot expect your audience to be!

■ Response: What do you want to achieve as a result of your presentation? What do you want people to do or think, understand or accept as a result of your presentation? Do you want colleagues to accept future sales forecasts? Or be persuaded to adopt a new product? How will you measure whether your presentation has fulfilled its aim?

Practical details:

1 **When will you speak?** How long will you speak for? Will there be time for questions?

2 **Where will you give the presentation?** For example, will there be a projector and screen if you want to prepare a Power-Point? What is the room like where you will speak?

3 **How are you going to make your presentation?** For example, how formal is it? Will you stand up or sit down?

4 **Why are you giving the presentation?** Why you? This will help you prepare not only the standard material but also your unique approach.

If you're not clear on your key message, you cannot expect your audience to be.

5.2

Think and plan creatively

The next stage is *not* yet to write; it is to think.

The best way to think creatively is to write about your thoughts in a pattern diagram sometimes called pattern notes, or Mind Map™. This is a diagram you creatively draw that captures all the main aspects of your central thoughts as you see them. To do this, you should:

■ Take a blank sheet of A4 paper, arranging it in landscape format.
■ Write the central thought or theme (a word or a few words, not a whole sentence) of your presentation in the middle of the paper.
■ Write around that central word other key words that relate to it.
■ Keep branching out various other aspects of the theme that come into your mind.
■ If you get stuck at any point, answer the question words *who?*, *why?*, *where?*, *what?*, *when?*, *how?* These will stimulate your thinking.
■ At this stage, do not reject any thoughts. (Use an eraser sparingly to delete what you have written.)
■ As a next stage you can draw lines to show the links from your central thought to your key words and between individual key words.
■ You can colour in different key words to show which ones are related.
■ You can number the different key words in order of importance. Later on, as you deal with each aspect in your writing, you can put a line through each one.

one minute wonder Probably the key words in your Mind Map™ are nouns. You could add powerful verbs and adjectives to make strong phrases that will be effective in your talk. For example, if you're giving a talk on effective presentations you could have such strong phrases as 'Prepare useful visual aids' and 'Expect positive and negative feedback'.

Aim for between three and five key messages in your presentation. If you have more than five you risk overloading your audience with too much information.

Five ways in which you can order your material:

1 Move from facts to a conclusion.

2 Start with a conclusion and see how that conclusion is supported by certain facts and arguments.

3 State your opinion, and then give arguments for and against that opinion, and finally draw conclusions.

4 State a particular situation and then present the various possible solutions, with their advantages and disadvantages.

5 Explain the different stages of a process.

Time spent thinking creatively is not wasted.

5.3

Work on your words

The words you say are the single most important part of your presentation. You need to work hard at the words of your presentation, varying your style and choosing your words carefully to keep your message simple and clear.

■ **Think what is the one key point** of what you are trying to say and break that down into a few (three to five) key messages. If you include more, you risk overloading your presentation. Less is more.

■ **Be specific.** Avoid general statements. Your presentation will have a greater impact if you discuss a particular example. If you are talking about diversity among a population then quoting an actual example of an event that celebrates diversity will be more effective than simply giving a list of different groups.

■ **Use variety.** The average length of time that someone can focus on spoken input is 20 minutes, so you need to use different ways to keep the attention, interest and motivation of your audience. This is especially important for meetings after lunch when sessions should be particularly dynamic to stop your audience's attention from drifting.

■ **Use short sentences.** When we write normal English, our sentences tend to be longer than when we speak. Keep your sentences to about 15 words.

■ **Use fewer abstract nouns and more verbs.** For example, change *conduct an investigation* to *investigate*; change *suffer a deterioration* to *deteriorate*.

■ **Use active verbs.** In the sentence, '*Caroline broke the window*', the verb *broke* is active: it is performed by the person who is named: Caroline. This contrasts with the sentence, '*The window was broken by Caroline*', in which the verb *broken* is passive: the window has an action done to it. *By Caroline* is optional: in a passive sentence, you do not need to say who has done the action. Passive verbs are longer and sound more formal; active verbs are shorter and sound more natural. They are also easier to understand, partly because a person is named early in the sentence. Use fewer passive verbs and more active verbs.

■ **Use short words.** Try to use words of one or two syllables. Listen to songs written by The Beatles; most of their lyrics consist of one- or two-syllable words. Try not to use formal words but words that we use in ordinary speech.

■ **Avoid jargon or clichés**, e.g. *going forward, downsizing, a level playing field*. Ask yourself or discuss with a colleague face-to-face (not by email) what you actually mean. Be ruthless with yourself to express yourself clearly and simply.

Think of the one key point of what you're trying to say and break that down into a few subpoints.

5.4

Plan your beginning, middle and end

Your introduction is your opportunity to make sure your audience knows what to expect. First impressions are vital. Your introduction needs to address five different topics. Conveniently, they spell out the word **INTRO**:

■ **Interest:** Raise interest in yourself and your topic. Give some background to yourself. Why is your topic relevant? And why are you qualified to talk about it? An example of a recent news story or YouTube video can make a good opener.

■ **Need:** Explain why your audience needs to listen to your presentation. Will it make their life easier? Will it make them richer? A clear, concise example of an organization or person you previously have helped can be useful here.

■ **Timing:** Tell your audience how long you will speak for. This is very helpful to mentally prepare your audience, particularly if they are worried they might miss lunch or a flight. Make sure you stick to your promised timing.

■ **Response:** Tell your audience how and when they can participate. Should they interrupt you while you speak? Will there be time for questions at the end?

■ **Objective:** This is when you tell your audience what the purpose and the scope of the presentation are. Don't be afraid of repeating yourself.

The middle of a presentation is like the meat in the sandwich. It is the key part of what you are saying. However, it may also be the point when your audience loses attention. Ways to maintain your audience's attention in the central part of your talk include:

■ **Varying the style** of what you are saying. Ask challenging questions. Express your message in a story. Quote an up-to-date event.
■ **Making sure your presentation is arranged logically**, that its points are ordered in such a way that one follows on naturally from the previous one.
■ **Making sure your evidence**, e.g. facts and figures, clearly supports your argument and is consistent with its conclusions.

Your conclusion may well be the part that remains with your audience for a long time afterwards.

■ **Begin with a signal** that you are now coming to the end. For example, say, 'Finally, let's draw all these thoughts together.'
■ **Your conclusion** should bring together all the key messages of your presentation up to that point. Restate your earlier key messages. Don't include any significantly new material in your conclusion.
■ **Emphasize the one key message** that you have tried to communicate in your presentation.
■ **Include a clear statement** of what response you would like members of your audience to make … what the next steps are that you want them to do. Say, 'The one thing I'd like you to take away from today is …' Be practical.
■ **End with a signal** that you have now finished. For example, say, 'Thank you for your attention. I'd now be very happy to answer your questions.'

5.5

Use PowerPoint wisely

Years ago, PowerPoint was cutting edge. Now, you need a good reason to use it; flip charts are fashionable again, as they are flexible and versatile, especially in an informal setting. If PowerPoint isn't adding anything to your presentation, then don't use it. And don't let PowerPoint ruin your presentation.

If you are using PowerPoint, then avoid these Seven Deadly PowerPoint Sins:

1 Don't use illegible text. Stick to large fonts (no more than six lines per page) and clearly distinguished colours (red on grey, yellow on blue, black on white).

case study I've found that using a combination of a few well-chosen words and an image that encapsulates the key idea visually works well. The words appeal to those in my audience who like words and the image will appeal to those who are more visually

2 Don't just write up what you are saying. People will read it instead of listening to you. Use the slides to *illustrate* your point but not to *make* your point.

3 Don't put too much text on the page. Keep your points simple. Avoid subpoints if possible.

4 Don't use distracting effects like fancy page-turn animations. The presentation is about what you have to say, not about your (lack of!) PowerPoint skills.

5 Don't be totally reliant on technology. Make sure you have a backup plan in case technology fails. Save your PowerPoint presentation in different versions of PowerPoint and put them on a memory stick, so that if your laptop fails, you can use another one.

6 Keep your eye contact with the audience, not the screen, and not the remote control.

7 Make sure you have time to arrive early and ensure that the technology works and, just as importantly, you know how to use it.

Don't put too many headings on slides; keep your points simple.

orientated and remain in their mind. Choosing the one key image that encapsulates the idea takes time but I'm sure it's worth it. An example: a picture of buttresses supporting a cathedral to communicate the concepts of strengthening and confirming.

5.6

Present tables and charts skilfully

If you're communicating anything relating to numbers, then you will probably want to show some kind of table, graph, chart or diagram. These can be very effective tools in presentations.

These styles of chart are popular in presentations:

■ **Bar chart.** Has bars of equal width but with different heights in proportion to the values they stand for. Useful for comparing quantities over time.

■ **Pie chart.** A circle divided into slices of differing sizes. Useful for comparing data in proportion to a whole, but can be difficult for the eye to take in quickly. Keep to a maximum of five slices.

■ **Gantt chart.** A type of bar chart that illustrates the duration of certain tasks over time. Useful for planning and scheduling.

■ **Flow chart.** Illustrates a series of steps and is useful to show the stages of a process.

■ **Line graph.** Shows the relationship between two kinds of information (along the vertical and horizontal axes) and how they vary depending on each other. Useful to show changes or trends over time.

Whatever style of table, chart, graph or diagram, bear in mind the following:

one minute wonder If you want to draw something on a flip chart, draw it in pencil first before the meeting then go over it with the pen during the actual meeting. Colleagues will be amazed at your drawing skills!

1 Don't include too much information; show only the key data. Keep your presentation clear, simple and uncluttered.

2 Use colour to make the graphs, tables, diagrams and charts more appealing and memorable. Also use clear titles, with concise subheadings and labels. Make sure that the numbers are large enough to be legible.

3 Bear in mind that people visually take in figures presented in columns more easily than those presented in rows. For example, if you are comparing data, put the numbers in adjacent columns, not rows.

4 Also for the sake of clarity, round numbers up or down to two digits, e.g. not 9.1637 and 8.43 but 9.2 and 8.4.

5 Finally, double-check your numbers. If someone spots that your percentages add up to 95% – or 105% – not only will you be embarrassed but you also might be forced on the spot to recalculate and explain how you came to make that error.

Illustrate numbers as simply as possible and make sure they add up.

5.7

Manage your nerves

Many speakers become nervous and tense before they give their presentation. Symptoms of nervousness include your breathing becoming shallow, your mouth drying up, having a feeling of nausea and your body becoming tense. The trick is to learn to work through it and overcome it.

You can overcome your nervousness by:

■ **Focusing** on something apart from yourself. Think about your audience. They probably won't detect your nervousness. Remember you probably know more than they do. Most of them want you to succeed and are on your side. Go through the key points of your message again in your mind.

■ **Breathing deeply.** I've found this the most helpful practical technique when I become tense. Taking long deep breaths in and out will naturally relax your body.

case study Recently Jia led a course on the character of a person who helped others. She was nervous before it started as it was with a group of people she didn't know well. Fortunately she had her notes, but she also had in her mind a word beginning with each

"There are two types of speakers, those that are nervous and those that are liars"

Mark Twain (1835–1910), American author

■ **Drinking water** or sipping water if you are so tense you cannot swallow properly. Don't drink alcohol.

■ **Giving yourself a pep talk.** You have a unique background with all the skills and experiences that have brought you to where you are now. Other people believe in you; believe in yourself.

■ **Trying to appear confident.** You *have* done your preparation. You *have* worked hard at your presentation. You have every right to see that all your hard work should make you look confident.

■ **Being practical.** Write out your beginning and end and memorize their key points. Arrive early. Practise your presentation in advance.

■ **Controlling your thoughts.** You've worked hard on your presentation; now work on your imagination. Visualize yourself going on the stage, speaking confidently, and your audience smiling and receiving your presentation warmly. This will challenge negative thoughts.

■ **Smiling a lot.** Reminding yourself of a funny joke or story may steady your nerves.

Don't give in to nervousness, but learn to work through it and overcome it.

of the first five letters of the alphabet: A attentive; B brave; C caring; D disciplined; E encouraging. Repeating these in her mind allowed her to concentrate on the delivery, rather than focusing on her nervousness.

5.8

Be aware of your body language

Alongside the words you use, body language is a very important part of how you communicate. Body language is the set of gestures and movements that are part of the way in which you communicate your presentation.

Ways in which your body language can help you in your presentation include:

■ **Stand up.** One of the most important elements of your body language is your posture. Time and again, research has shown that standing up is the most effective way to achieve this goal. You are best off standing with your feet firmly planted apart.

- **Standing up** will also make you more visible to your audience. But make sure you're visible to everyone. Check there aren't any blind spots from where people won't be able to see you.
- **Don't speak with your back to the audience** while looking at the screen or writing on a flip chart; they will pay less attention to you.

■ **Keep eye contact with your audience.** Because you're confident of your presentation, you will not need to look at your notes all the time, so you can focus your attention on members of your audience.

- **Look at all your audience.** Don't focus on one part of your audience, but make sure that, over time, you look throughout the audience.
- **Don't stare.** Don't look for too long at any one individual, as that will make them feel uncomfortable.
- **Be confident in the style** you feel comfortable with when presenting. I don't feel comfortable talking all the time when I am presenting; I like to ask questions to see whether my audience is in tune with what I am saying.

■ **Move around a little.** It's all too easy to give your presentation standing still and from behind a lectern. Moving around the room a little is a useful way of keeping the attention of your audience.

- **Don't 'hide behind' the lectern.** Also, don't grip the lectern to steady your nerves. Come out from your safe comfort zone; move out from behind the lectern and walk around the room a little, engaging eye contact with members of your audience.
- **Keep smiling.** Smiling will make your audience feel you're relaxed, even if you aren't. It will also relax your audience.
- **Use your hands** and other gestures that come to you naturally to emphasize your key points, to push points home and to connect with your audience. (Learn from the hand gestures of TV weather forecasters.)
- **Avoid distracting habits.** Don't play with your hair, jangle keys, play with jewellery or a flip-chart pen, or jingle coins.

Don't keep looking at your notes, but make good eye contact with your audience.

5.9

Control your voice

Your voice is the single most important aspect that you have in giving your presentation. Learn how to use it well to make your presentation effective.

You can learn how to exercise control over your voice as you are speaking. Practise voice control; learn how to breathe deeply – not just raising your shoulders. When you breathe in deeply, you should feel your lower ribs move upwards and air build up in your lungs. Allow the greater force of air to go through the larynx (voice box) at the back of your throat and produce a louder voice.

Before a presentation, warm up your voice. Hum; talk to yourself – but make sure no one is around to hear you!

Here are some guidelines to follow in your presentation:

■ **Vary the volume** with which you speak: sometimes loudly, sometimes softly.
■ **Vary the speed** at which you speak: speak sometimes quickly, sometimes slowly.
■ **Add a range of tones** to your words. Don't speak with the same monotone all the time. Sound enthusiastic – your audience will pick this up.
■ **Open your mouth wide** and move your lips, articulating the words clearly and fully; don't slur syllables.

■ **Make sure your voice** doesn't drop at the end of sentences.

■ **Emphasize the positive words** you want to stress. You could even repeat them to highlight them further.

■ **Watch out for the meaningless fillers** that we all use: 'OK', 'you know', 'um', 'just'. Ask a friend to identify those that are your particular weakness. Once during a presentation, I counted how many times the speaker said 'um': 114 times in 45 minutes. It is better to be silent than to keep using fillers in this way.

Learn how to breathe deeply and practise voice control.

5.10

Deal with questions

Decide if you're happy to take questions during your presentation or if you would prefer them at the end.

Here are some helpful tips on answering questions:

■ **Identify likely questions** in your preparation and work out your response in advance.

■ **Sit down when listening to a question.** Stand up as you begin to answer it. (This will give you a little more time to think of the answer.) Taking a drink of water will also give you more time.

■ **Listen carefully to the question.** Don't interrupt the questioner. Write down key words in their question or as you plan your response and to help you concentrate.

■ **Use the person's name** in your response, 'Thank you, Robert.'

■ **Rephrase the question** before you begin your answer. Look at both the questioner and the wider audience as you do so. Rephrasing the question means that the whole audience will hear the question; it

case study Jill learnt that when replying to an awkward question, she shouldn't give her full eye contact to the questioner. She learnt to give about a quarter of her eye-contact time to that person, and about three-quarters to the rest of the audience. She

will also clarify it in your own mind and give you further time to work out how to answer it.

■ **Make sure you give some response** to the question that is asked. Do not follow the politician's method, however, of not answering the question.

■ **Use the opportunity** to repeat your key messages.

■ **If you don't know the answer** to the question, then be honest and say so. You could offer to check out the details and respond to the questioner later or ask a colleague who is present at the meeting and who you know is more expert in that area to respond. Don't try to bluff your way through it, pretending to answer a question when you can't. It will show.

Identify likely questions and your responses as part of your preparation.

knew that if she gave her full eye-contact time to the hostile questioner, they would then take that as permission to continue to ask questions, which she wanted to avoid.

Taking part in a meeting

Everyone has a role to play in a meeting. You may not be chairing a meeting or taking minutes but you are attending it and so the part you play is still important.

In this chapter, we'll consider such key skills as remembering colleagues' names, improving your listening, speaking persuasively and discussing positively. If you're conducting negotiations then you will want to close the deal successfully. Finally, we consider how to make sure your phone calls and video conferences are effective and also how to revive your meeting if it needs new life.

6.1

Participate actively

If you don't have a particular role in a meeting such as chairing or taking minutes, don't be tempted to think you can just sit back; everyone who attends a meeting has an important part to play in ensuring it is successful.

Before the meeting:

Arrive before the meeting is due to begin so that it can start punctually. Before the meeting, prepare yourself by reading all the relevant reports and background papers. Make notes of the points you want to make during the meeting.

If necessary, alert the chair before the meeting to any significant points you want to raise that might be considered controversial in order to minimize any difficulties in the actual meeting.

During the meeting:

It can be helpful to consider the different participants in the meeting as members of a team. We can spell this out:

■ **Team.** In a team, everyone is aware of the different roles and responsibilities of the other members. Respect and trust between different members of the team are vital. Good communication among the team is essential. Timing is important: know when to express your opinion and when to remain silent.

■ **Effort.** Being a member of a team requires hard work as you all work together to achieve a common goal. Similarly, in a meeting you need to work hard by concentrating throughout the meeting, not being distracted but maintaining your interest, listening well and then speaking at appropriate times.

■ **Authority.** Be aware of the level of authority you personally have to make decisions in the meeting. If you're representing a department, check with your boss what authority you have in the meeting. For example, do you have the right to agree to spend a certain amount of money?

■ **Maturity.** You may be just setting out as a junior manager, but it's important to show that you're trustworthy in small matters. Your bosses will notice that you're reliable in dealing with relatively simple issues and will gradually give you increasing responsibilities.

Each participant shares in the responsibility of the success or failure of the meeting. You cannot reasonably leave a meeting saying that it was a waste of time. If the meeting has been a failure, you yourself are partly to blame. It's far better to take an active, positive role in a meeting and be responsible by playing your part to the full.

Even if you don't have a particular role in a meeting, you still need to play your part fully.

6.2

Remember names

Many of us find it difficult to remember people's names. We recognize a familiar face and want to greet the colleague with their name but find that it escapes us.

Here are a few tips on how to remember names:

■ **Prepare yourself.** Be mentally alert when someone says their name. Listen closely. Concentrate on the sounds of the name as the person says it.

■ **Don't be afraid to ask someone to repeat their name**, 'I'm sorry, I didn't quite catch that?' You could always say the name back to the person to check that you have pronounced it right. The more often you repeat the name, the more likely you are to remember it.

■ **Write names down.** I find this helpful. As soon as I meet someone new and have found out their name I try to write it down. If you don't know how to spell their name, you can write it down using a phonetic (or your own spelling) system. Putting it down on paper will help you remember it. Of course, you need to do this unobtrusively and out of sight of the person concerned. It can be done easily in meetings.

■ **Use people's names** when addressing them. 'Thanks, Peter, that's very helpful.' Beware of overdoing this: to use someone's name every time you speak to them is excessive.

■ **Be realistic.** If you are joining a new committee, you can be overwhelmed by having to learn the names of every other person. What is realistic, however, is to learn the name of one different person each time the meeting takes place.

■ **Associate a feature** with a particular image. If Brenda is blonde, you can think of Brenda for both blonde and Brenda. Notice the person's hairstyle, nose, teeth, smile, eyebrows or cheeks. An acquaintance has slightly protruding upper teeth, so I think of *dental* and *Dave*. The face of a man at a conference reminded me of a Coca-Cola bottle, so I used that to remember his name, Mr Coles (Cola/Coles).

■ **Put names in alphabetical order** in your mind. This is a personal one as I write dictionaries, but if I have Julie, June and Karen sitting next to each other in a meeting then I can remember their names more easily.

Actively concentrate as you meet someone for the first time and they tell you their name.

6.3

Think creatively

Many colleagues find the technique of brainstorming[2] very useful to think creatively or solve problems to discuss the issues around a certain question. It can offer a fresh approach to generate new ideas, solve a problem or research a subject.

■ Choose one person to write points on a flip chart or whiteboard.

■ Write the central issue in the middle of the paper or board.

■ Invite colleagues to suggest ideas that arise from the issue, which should then be written down.

■ Be creative and imaginative. Involve everyone. No idea is rejected; no one's input is criticized but each person's contribution is considered valid. All ideas and suggestions should be written down, whether they seem sensible or strange.

■ Continue to make suggestions, ideally building on the ones already offered and written down.

■ If you get stuck at any point, answer the question words: *who?*, *why?*, *where?*, *what?*, *when?*, *how?* (and add *how much?* and *how many?*). These will stimulate your thinking.

■ Use symbols, images or pictures if you find them helpful.

2 Also called 'thought showers'.

■ Look at what you have written down. Discuss what the key issues are. Sort the different points and analyse them. Link different issues by highlighting them in various colours, e.g. green for relationship issues, blue for strategic matters.

■ Join together linked issues, refining the key points. Put elements that now seem weaker under stronger categories.

■ Agree actions, e.g. 'next (immediate) follow-up steps', and medium- and long-term plans that you are going to pursue.

Let your imagination stimulate you and your colleagues and you will be able to capture the different aspects of a subject.

6.4

Listen well

When we think of communication skills, we often tend to think only of speaking, but listening is at least as important as speaking. It has been said that we have one mouth but two ears, so maybe we should spend twice as much time listening as speaking.

In a meeting, listening well means that you will:

■ understand your fellow participants' point of view. When you know someone's opinion, you can respond more effectively than if you just say something without thinking about what they are saying. The ideal is that in a meeting, the input of the various participants should build on one another to achieve a constructive discussion and reach agreement.

■ concentrate on what the other person or people are saying. Often you may find yourself planning in your mind what you are going to say instead of listening to the other person. If you listen well, focus on (e.g. by making good eye contact with) the person you are listening to.

■ discern the main points being discussed. Sometimes it takes a while for the real core issues to emerge in a meeting. For example, are certain assumptions being made? Are such assumptions valid?

■ be able to distinguish between facts and someone's opinions on those facts.

■ find that sometimes you don't understand what someone is saying. Perhaps they're not expressing themselves clearly or the subject is unfamiliar to you. Here, you need to ask a question to clarify what the person meant. You may be afraid to ask what you might think of as a basic question, but be courageous and ask. You will probably find that the question is also in the minds of others in the meeting but they are afraid to ask.

■ not be distracted by wandering thoughts.

■ be open to changing your mind on a subject. You may have come into the meeting with a set opinion, but if you listen with an open mind, the different thoughts you hear may lead you to revise your opinion or make a different decision from the one you originally thought of.

Listening is hard work. But if you listen well, you will show that you respect and value the person or people you are listening to.

6.5

Speak persuasively

In a meeting, you should work out in advance what you want. You should prepare what you're going to say in order to convince and persuade the other participants. In particular, you should know clearly the point you want the meeting to have reached by the end of the discussion.

In your preparation and presentation, you need to:

■ Express your main point as clearly as you can. Be as simple as possible. Work hard to express yourself in a way that the other participants will understand. That is your main aim, rather than impressing your fellow participants with words you barely understand yourself.
■ Present your points logically. Work hard to state your explanation in a structured, organized and step-by-step manner. If you do this, it will help if you need to gain the agreement of the meeting on each particular point.

case study Jake was a salesman. He learnt that in trying to persuade people the words he chose mattered. He learnt to use such positive words as *you, we, us* and *together* to establish a good rapport. He

- Appeal to your audience's aims and aspirations.
- Think what your own unique contribution is. You may have a particular insight from an experience you have had.
- State the reasons for your point of view. Anticipate likely objections that might arise in the minds of your fellow participants. For example, give the reasons for and against a particular course of action or its advantages and disadvantages. What benefits would come? What difficulties?
- Be as simple as you can. Some colleagues make matters complicated and difficult to understand. Explain the steps as simply as possible.
- Make sure what you say is relevant to your main points. Exclude all that is not central to the issues you want to communicate, however interesting it may seem.
- Give examples (case studies), statistics (data) and/or quotations to support your points. Such additional material will act as evidence to help form the basis for the decision you want the participants to make.
- Finally, sum up by repeating your main points and drawing conclusions. Be clear about what the next step is that you want the participants to make, e.g. to decide on spending a certain amount of money.

Thinking about the next meeting at which you will speak, work out precisely what you want to achieve. What point do you want the participants to have reached by the end of the meeting?

also sometimes used such words as *discover, enjoy, exciting, new, save* and *special* to communicate strongly when trying to sell to customers.

6.6

Discuss positively

In a meeting, you may be tempted to be negative and disagree with what is being discussed. While there is a place for disagreement, you should do all you can to keep the atmosphere of the meeting positive.

In discussions in a meeting:

■ Respect other people even when you disagree with them. Instead of criticizing them personally, deal politely with the opinion, issue or objection that they have pointed out. Make sure you're not a colleague who is known for frequently being awkward, aggressive or antagonistic, one who constantly finds fault with everyone and everything or is known for always raising negative aspects or disadvantages.

■ Be positive and seek to be constructive. If a disagreement arises, try to be a peacemaker. Listen to the points raised by the different sides until the different parties feel listened to, and then play your part in seeking creatively to find a solution that will satisfy both sides.

■ Be open to changing your mind.

■ Realize there are some issues that are not worth disagreeing about. Save your energy for issues that are significant.

■ If the issue is serious, then have a quiet word with the chair of the meeting after the meeting has finished. Often you may not be aware of certain facts or the situation as a whole, which if you knew about would mean that you would change your point of view.

"Discussion is an exchange of knowledge; argument is an exchange of ignorance"

Robert Quillen (1887-1948), American humorist

■ Remain enthusiastic. Some colleagues in organizations are cynical. Rather than joining them, do your best to be committed and motivated. Just as a lack of enthusiasm is contagious, so is the presence of enthusiasm. Try it! When relationships are good in a company or organization, people work together effectively and the results are outstanding.

■ Finish the meeting on a positive note. I've been in too many meetings where the final point has been negative and people leave feeling discouraged. It is far better to end a meeting having dealt with a subject that leaves colleagues feeling highly motivated.

6.7

Conduct your negotiations

In Secret 2.5 we discussed preparing for negotiations. You will know in advance of the actual negotiations what authority you have to make decisions, what you are aiming at as your ideal agreement and what you are willing to accept as the best alternative if you cannot achieve your ideal.

How to conduct your negotiations:

■ State firmly your opening position. For example, if you are selling, state a high price and be willing to negotiate downwards; if you are buying, state a low price and be willing to increase it.
■ Continue to ask questions to find out what issues are important to the other side.
■ Allow the other side to answer. Listen carefully to their answers. A publisher once told me, 'We don't usually pay an advance.' I picked up on the word 'usually' and asked them about it: under what circumstances would they pay an advance? Over the years a relationship of trust developed between us as I worked well with them on several projects and later they paid an advance. My listening well paid off in the end.

"There is a danger in being persuaded before one understands"

(Thomas) Woodrow Wilson (1856–1924), US President

■ Concentrate on the issues that both sides agree on.

■ Hopefully before the meeting you will have considered what points you are willing to make compromises on, the points you are prepared to concede if necessary. Begin to discuss such variables, e.g. 'We might be willing to be flexible and offer an earlier delivery date if you were willing to be flexible on price.'

■ Don't make concessions too easily.

■ Imagine that you are in their situation. For example, if you were late delivering products last time, how will they feel? What guarantees can you give that you will deliver on time on this occasion?

■ As you progress through the negotiations, continue to summarize the points that both sides have accepted and agreed and make further suggestions.

■ If possible, think of different ways of achieving your goals. For example, 'We could offer you a three-year deal if you pay us a higher amount [state the exact sum] as an initial payment.'

■ Show that you're willing to make some concessions; give the other side something in exchange for something you need or want. Remain firm on what is non-negotiable, however.

At the end, close the deal: see Secret 6.8.

Work out before your meeting what is negotiable and what isn't.

6.8

Finalize your negotiations

As you complete your negotiations, you need to close the deal, i.e. gain the agreement of both sides to what has been discussed.

■ Use the existing situation to your advantage. If you find yourself in the fortunate position of agreeing the major points of a negotiation fairly quickly, then don't delay; the other side may change their mind.

■ Confirm explicitly the agreement you've reached, e.g. by saying, 'So you're happy with …?'

■ If you have an order form available on hard copy or digitally, then fill in their order there and then. Confirm the points agreed as soon as possible; for example, by issuing a contract that both sides will sign to show their agreement. Deal with any outstanding small details.

■ Now is not the time to be shy or timid. Equally, there is no need to be forceful or aggressive. Be true to yourself and the relationship you

---

case study Early on in my career, I was shy about closing the deal. I thought, 'What if they don't want to proceed?' Gradually, I learnt that one of the main points about negotiating is the relationship I have with the other side. Fortunately, the good relationship I had

have developed with your colleagues on the other side. Assert yourself clearly and confidently; for example, by saying, 'Are we OK to go ahead on the basis of what we've just agreed?'

■ Be sure you can communicate the points you have agreed with your colleagues. They would not want to feel that you have betrayed them in any way.

built up with the other side before I had begun negotiating meant that although I may have felt awkward about closing the deal, the negotiations themselves were ultimately successful.

6.9

A phone call is a meeting

Have you ever made a phone call, ended the call and then thought, 'I forgot to mention (a certain point)?' You could avoid that by remembering that a phone call is in a sense a meeting. You could therefore write down before you make the call the points you want to discuss during your conversation and look at your list during the call.

In the light of the fact that your phone conversation is a meeting then you should:

■ Email the colleague in advance to arrange a time for the conversation that is convenient to both of you.

■ Write down on paper or electronically a list of the points you want to discuss during the conversation. While you are speaking in the phone call, you can then write alongside your points what you are discussing and agreeing.

■ If you have, for example, three issues to discuss and one of them is most important, then discuss that one first. This is in case the colleague has to leave suddenly and then you find you don't have time to discuss the particular point you wanted to. This could be a great disappointment to you, because you may have spent a long time trying to contact them in the first place.

■ Speak as simply and clearly as possible, especially if the native language of the colleague at the other end of the phone is not the same as yours. Work hard at breaking down what you're trying to say into simple steps.

■ If you have to discuss several issues, one of which is delicate, signal that fact at the beginning of the conversation by saying, for example, 'Mary, as you know we've got several points to discuss. One of them is slightly sensitive and we'll come to that in a few minutes.' Signalling that in advance gives you the opportunity in the first part of the conversation to develop a good relationship with your colleague, which you can then build on when you come to discuss the delicate issue.

■ Summarize what you have agreed at the end of each point and again at the end of your conversation.

■ After the conversation is finished, confirm in an email what you have both agreed. You could even draft the email before you begin the conversation and then send it shortly after completing the conversation.

Before you make a phone call, write down the points you want to discuss during the conversation.

6.10

Video conferencing

The benefits of video conferencing mean that you allow participants at several different locations to see one another and talk together face to face in a 'virtual' meeting. You can also make more efficient use of time, avoiding the need to spend time and resources on travel.

In video conferencing, you will need to:

■ **Confirm the time** of the meeting, especially if this involves different world time zones.

■ **Schedule the meeting** in a room with a good appearance and acoustics.

■ **Clear the room** of any distracting objects, e.g. bags, that could restrict the view or distract participants in other locations. Make sure all mobile phones are switched off.

■ **Make sure all equipment** – camera, projector, screen, microphones, loudspeakers and Internet connections are all working properly. Don't put your laptop next to the microphone as the fan will generate noise and disrupt the meeting.

■ **Work out a clear agenda** for your meeting in advance, noting who will do what, and circulating that to all participants in advance. Clarify who will chair the meeting, introduce participants, etc. Work out in advance how graphics will be sent or shared.

■ **Put name cards** clearly in front of individuals, and say your name as you begin to speak.

■ **Speak clearly** and not too fast. Ask questions to a particular participant: 'This is a question for —'.

■ **Listen;** don't interrupt while someone else is speaking. Don't engage in conversations with other participants while a colleague is talking.

■ **Make sure a translator** is available if necessary.

■ **Minimize possible interruptions.** Think through what might happen (e.g. fire-alarm tests?) to minimize possible interruptions.

■ **Make sure participants** face the camera while talking.

■ **Remember there may be a slight time delay** that can lead to people trying to talk at the same time. If you are giving a presentation, get everyone to go on 'mute'.

Video conferencing makes more efficient use of time, avoiding the need to spend time and resources on travel, but needs careful planning.

6.11

Revive your meeting

Most groups go through times when the participants are not enthusiastic or are bored. Here are three tips as to how to fight against general apathy and lack of enthusiasm and bring new life into your meeting.

1 Ask yourself, 'Is the meeting really necessary?' Are you holding the meeting simply for its own sake? Has the meeting lost its sense of direction and purpose? Too many meetings are simply about planning other meetings.

- Only hold the meeting when it's necessary to discuss a particular issue.
- When sending out the agenda, the chair could include an explanation to emphasize the purpose and focus of the meeting.
- You may even come to the radical decision that the meetings of the group should no longer continue and the group should stop meeting. Be courageous and see if anyone notices!

2 Do something different. Here are some suggestions:

- ask someone else to chair the meeting
- bring in new members

- change the venue of the meeting
- bring in refreshments
- change the order of items you discuss
- shorten the length of the meeting. If it usually lasts two hours, then try to fit everything into one hour
- ask the participants to remain standing if the meeting is brief
- draw your agenda as a graphic

3 Give each participant a particular role to play, i.e. give them some responsibility for following up a particular point or starting, continuing or completing a project. They will then need to report back to the next meeting on their progress. Giving participants responsibility may reduce their negative emotions and encourage them to be more positive.

If the meeting has lost its sense of direction and purpose, it may be time to be courageous and disband it.

After the meeting

You've worked hard at the meeting ... all the preparation beforehand and then during the meeting ... so now don't allow it all to be wasted. You need to implement and communicate the meeting's action points, keep up momentum and make good progress, ensuring that working relationships remain strong.

7.1

Communicate decisions well

After the meeting has finished, you need to implement the decisions made and communicate the decisions to the different groups of people involved.

■ Make your action points SMART. Look back at Secret 3.5.
■ Communicate clearly. Discuss and agree during the meeting who will communicate the various decisions when the meeting has finished.

- discuss and agree precisely who will communicate with whom
- discuss and agree precisely what you will communicate
- discuss and agree when you will communicate the decision

case study I once led a team of 100 people to work on a large reference book. I divided the 100 colleagues into ten teams and appointed a team leader in charge of each team. I knew there would be difficulties of some kind during the project so I deliberately spent some time at the start of the project getting to know the team leaders in face-to-face meetings. Sure enough, within a few months we ran into difficulties.

■ Inform colleagues who were not present at the meeting about any actions that they need to pursue or that affect them.

■ Work out the best way of communicating most effectively with colleagues: the choice will probably be between email, phone calls or face-to-face meetings.

- email is cheapest, then phone calls, with face-to-face being the most expensive.
- for some, a phone call to say, for example, 'We've got the contract,' is good, which may then be followed up by an email giving greater detail.
- face-to-face is the best way to build relationships, e.g. at the beginning of a project, or to discuss difficult or sensitive matters, but this is the most expensive.

■ At the beginning of a business relationship, it can be helpful to discuss the best way of working with a colleague. For example, some colleagues may prefer phone calls (in which case, agree a time that is convenient to both parties); others may prefer email.

Work out the most effective way to communicate the points that have been agreed.

These were not insurmountable, however, and we overcame them and eventually brought the project to a successful conclusion. By communicating well and spending time in face-to-face meetings with the key individuals in the early stages of the project, I had developed a store of goodwill that enabled us to survive the difficulties.

7.2

Move forward

You will have reached certain decisions at a meeting. Now is the time to make sure you put them into action.

■ If you're delegating work, divide up the task into smaller, more manageable tasks.

- Give written instructions; often you can 'cut and paste' from the minutes of the meeting or at least use them as a basis for your instructions.
- Give other instructions as relevant, e.g. if you want a colleague to write a report, state your expectations of the length of the report they should write, e.g. two or ten pages.
- Be clear as to when you want the work completed by.
- At the end, to check that the person you have delegated work to has understood your instructions; don't ask them, 'Have you understood what you have to do?' That would probably lead to a nod of the head to indicate yes. A better way is to ask them to explain to you what they should do. Their response will show their level of understanding.

case study I was secretary of a charity for several years. After panicking in my first year, I thought I would be working in that role for several years so I decided to become more organized. I set up a spreadsheet of the dates of all the different meetings and put the recurring

■ Agree any outstanding details and confirm these in writing.

- For formal matters, write a contract and obtain their signature on hard copy or electronic versions.
- Confirm commitments that have been agreed earlier. For example, if a colleague has said they will help you once a project is underway, check (with them and/or their boss, as relevant) that they are still willing and able to be involved.

■ Begin to implement your decision. Hopefully, before the meeting, you will already have worked out the next step(s) to be undertaken once the decision has been made.

■ Tackle any difficult issues that emerged at the meeting. Don't wait till the next meeting before doing this, but make a start in dealing with them between meetings.

■ Consolidate the progress made in meetings later by sending informal follow-up emails, to check that the action points are being pursued successfully.

■ At the end, thank the colleague for completing the task that was delegated.

What is the next step you need to take to follow up a meeting you've recently attended?

items that needed to take place against the dates. I then realized that there were gaps and I could introduce new ideas at those meetings. By organizing the dates well, I managed the role effectively and was able to help the charity move forward.

7.3

Keep up momentum between meetings

The time between meetings is not the time to sit back and do nothing. It is the time to be active, busily working out and following up the points agreed during the meeting and preparing for the next one.

Between meetings, you should:

■ Look back at what was agreed during the previous meeting:

- Check the actions agreed at the meeting that you were responsible for. Make sure you complete them by the time agreed at the meeting. If you're unsure about (or have forgotten!) exactly what you should be doing, then contact the chair or another trusted member who was present at the meeting.
- If you are the chair or hold another key position in the leadership of the meeting, then make sure that the important actions are being followed through properly. It is possible that the action involved might change slightly from that agreed at the meeting. This is probably all right, as long as there is basic movement forward and the chair of the meeting agrees with the adjusted direction being pursued.

"If you are planning for one year, plant rice. If you are planning for ten years, plant trees. If you are planning for 100 years, plant people"

Indian proverb

- The results of the follow-up of points agreed at the previous meeting will be considered during the 'Matters arising' section of the next meeting, so make sure that they are completed thoroughly: deal with any details that remain outstanding.

■ Look forward to the next meeting:

- This is both in terms of the regular items on the agenda, e.g. progress reports. You should therefore monitor carefully your schedules and costs and also control the quality of your products and/or services. See also Secret 7.4.
- Prepare for fresh initiatives and new directions that the next meeting might want to pursue. You could do the groundwork for these in consultation with the chair to bring proposals to the next meeting.
- Look forward into the future. Prepare all the time for what is coming up. This might be two or three meetings away, but you still need to arrange meetings between key people and put certain actions in place now, to ensure that something is successful several months later.

Make sure you complete your action points from the previous meeting on time.

7.4

Check your progress regularly

Between meetings, you need to make sure that you apply effective monitoring controls to constantly check the key aspects of your work. If you don't have such thorough controls and procedures in place, you won't know where you are or whether the decisions made at a meeting are being implemented successfully.

We can use the example of a project to illustrate such checks. In a project, you need to monitor closely:

■ Time

- Is the work proceeding according to the agreed schedule or are you running late?
- If you can see that the project is running late, then contact other colleagues to help work on the project to get it back on track.
- Check your timings against the original agreed schedule and note and explain any variations from that schedule.
- Beware 'scope creep', a series of small gradual changes that together cause delay to a project.

■ Cost

- Is your expenditure under control, or is it unrestricted?
- Is your income on track according to your forecasts?
- Check all your figures against your projected budget and note and explain any variations from the budget.
- Check your actual cash flow, i.e. that you have sufficient funds available to make the payments that have been agreed.
- Develop a procurement policy (procedures in your company or organization to buy goods and services), in which colleagues have authority to spend up to a certain amount without checking with their boss.
- Make sure that costs are allocated to certain specified cost centres to keep track of the costs incurred.

■ Quality

- Is what you are producing, whether it is a physical product or a service, at the required quality?
- Of the three key items, time, cost and quality, quality is the most difficult to measure. However, because it is difficult to quantify, you need to work especially hard at quality controls, i.e. objective criteria that will measure quality.
- If your product isn't at the desired quality, outside companies may turn away from you to your competitors to fulfil their requirements.

Time, cost, quality: which do you need to deal with more effectively?

7.5

Maintain good relationships

During your meetings, it may become clear that relationships between some of the participants may be poor or strained.

Ways in which you can maintain good relationships (rapport) between colleagues at work include:

■ Develop your own personal qualities.

- Do you have integrity? Are you honest and firm in your principles? Or are you hypocritical, claiming that you are better than you really are? Are you fair and honest?
- Are you committed in your work? Don't just do the minimum necessary.
- How trustworthy are you? Other people are likely to trust you more if you yourself can be depended on. Do you keep the promises you make? For example, if you cannot do something by a certain time, don't say that you can.

■ Respect others even when you disagree with them.

- Respecting others will mean that you support them in public. If you need to deal with issues between you, then do so privately.

"The most important single ingredient in the formula of success is knowing how to get along with people"

Theodore Roosevelt (1858–1919), US President

- Respecting others will mean that you do not blame them publicly.

■ **If you need to deal with conflict** then it can be helpful to take the following steps. These should be undertaken face-to-face, not by email!

- Discern what the real issues are. Listen – really listen – to what colleagues have to say.
- If necessary, listen to the stories/accounts of an incident from each different person involved.
- If necessary, write notes (with the person's permission) so that you can record what is being said.
- Distinguish (1) the issue itself, (2) the feelings (e.g. anger) that the issue has raised and (3) issues of identity, e.g. a person feeling emotionally threatened by someone else's behaviour.
- Consider constructive, creative ways of solving the difficulty: suggest and discuss those with the different sides.

Do all you can to build strong working relationships.

7.6

Evaluate your meeting

You need to learn lessons for the future by looking back at the experience of the meeting.

Consider what worked successfully and what didn't go so well:

■ In preparation for your meeting:

- Was the agenda circulated in good time?
- Were the key people invited?
- Were the practical arrangements satisfactory?
- Were technical matters, e.g. projection of PowerPoints by laptop and projector, well set up?
- Did the chair and the minute-taker discuss the running of the meeting, e.g. did the chair alert the minute-taker to any difficult issues that were likely to arise?

■ At the beginning of your meeting:

- Did the chair welcome everyone and introduce newcomers?
- Did the chair announce the key purpose of the meeting?

■ During your meeting:

- Did the chair lead the meeting effectively?
- Did the meeting go on too long?

- Did the chair keep to the agenda and maintain close control over who spoke?
- Did the chair motivate the participants?
- Did all the participants take part well?
- Were the presentations given clear and neither too long nor too short?
- Did the chair summarize the discussions well and reach firm conclusions?
- Did the meeting make wise decisions based on the evidence presented?
- Were the decisions reached SMART, i.e. Specific, Measurable, Agreed, Realistic and Timed?

■ After your meeting:

- Were the minutes of the meeting written up, checked by the chair and circulated promptly? Were the decisions that were reached during the meeting communicated well and promptly to the relevant colleagues?
- Were the actions agreed during the meeting followed through satisfactorily?
- Were any difficult or strained relationships that emerged during the meeting improved as far as possible?

Think of three things about your meeting that worked well. Now think of one thing that didn't go well. What practical steps will you take to make sure that the one thing will go better next time?

Jargon buster

Agenda
The list of items to be discussed at a meeting.

AOB
Any other business on the agenda of a meeting.

Brainstorming
(Also called 'thought showers'.) The act of colleagues creatively offering suggestions to generate new ideas, solve a problem or research a subject.

Breakout
A small group of people who are separate from a larger group in a meeting for a discussion on their own.

Chair
The person who leads the meeting; chairman or chairwoman.

Close the deal
To reach a business agreement successfully.

Concession
A point that you give way on in negotiation.

Consensus
General agreement in reaching a decision.

DONM
Date of next meeting; an item at the end of an agenda.

Key Performance Indicators (KPIs)
Measurements used to evaluate how successful a company or organization is.

Matters arising
Points that have arisen from the last meeting; an item on the agenda.

Mind Map™
A diagram that organizes ideas, words, etc. around a central key word or idea; developed by Tony Buzan and widely used around the world.

Minutes
The official record of who was present at a meeting, the decisions that were agreed and the action points to be followed up.

Outcomes
The results you want from a meeting.

Overheads
The general business expenses of a company or organization.

Procurement
The processes and procedures in a company or organization to buy goods and services.

Quick win
An action that produces immediate visible benefits and can be implemented relatively easily and quickly.

Rapport
Good relationships with people.

Scope creep
A series of small gradual changes that together cause delay to a project.

Stakeholder
An individual who is directly or indirectly affected by an action, policy or project.

Virtual meeting
A meeting in which the participants are not physically present in the same place but one that is facilitated by computers.

Further reading

Websites

www.belbin.com

www.businessballs.com

www.businessknowhow.com

www.mindtools.com

www.thinkbuzan.com

Books by Martin Manser

Business Secrets: Mindpower (Harper Collins, 2010)
ISBN 978-0-00734-676-9

Business Secrets: Presenting (Harper Collins, 2010)
ISBN 978-0-00732-447-7

Business Secrets: Time Management (Harper Collins, 2010)
ISBN 978-0-0-0732-446-0

Introducing Management in a Week (Hodder and Stoughton, 2012)
ISBN 978-1-44415-961-5

Successful Business Communication in a Week (Hodder and Stoughton, 2013)
ISBN 978-144417-894-4

Successful Decision Making in a Week (Hodder and Stoughton, 2013)
ISBN 978-1-44418-041-1

Courses by Martin Manser

martinmanser.co.uk/courses